American
Trucks
of the 1950s

VELOCE

Also from Veloce Publishing –

Those Were The Days ... Series
Alpine Trials & Rallies 1910-1973 (Pfundner)
American 'Independent' Automakers – AMC to Willys 1945 to 1960 (Mort)
American Station Wagons – The Golden Era 1950-1975 (Mort)
American Trucks of the 1950s (Mort)
American Trucks of the 1960s (Mort)
American Woodies 1928-1953 (Mort)
Anglo-American Cars from the 1930s to the 1970s (Mort)
Austerity Motoring (Bobbitt)
Austins, The last real (Peck)
Brighton National Speed Trials (Gardiner)
British and European Trucks of the 1970s (Peck)
British Drag Racing – The early years (Pettitt)
British Lorries of the 1950s (Bobbitt)
British Lorries of the 1960s (Bobbitt)
British Touring Car Racing (Collins)
British Police Cars (Walker)
British Woodies (Peck)
Café Racer Phenomenon, The (Walker)
Don Hayter's MGB Story – The birth of the MGB in MG's Abingdon Design & Development Office (Hayter)
Drag Bike Racing in Britain – From the mid '60s to the mid '80s (Lee)
Dune Buggy Phenomenon, The (Hale)
Dune Buggy Phenomenon Volume 2, The (Hale)

Endurance Racing at Silverstone in the 1970s & 1980s (Parker)
Hot Rod & Stock Car Racing in Britain in the 1980s (Neil)
Mercedes-Benz Trucks (Peck)
MG's Abingdon Factory (Moylan)
Motor Racing at Brands Hatch in the Seventies (Parker)
Motor Racing at Brands Hatch in the Eighties (Parker)
Motor Racing at Crystal Palace (Collins)
Motor Racing at Goodwood in the Sixties (Gardiner)
Motor Racing at Nassau in the 1950s & 1960s (O'Neil)
Motor Racing at Oulton Park in the 1960s (McFadyen)
Motor Racing at Oulton Park in the 1970s (McFadyen)
Motor Racing at Thruxton in the 1970s (Grant-Braham)
Motor Racing at Thruxton in the 1980s (Grant-Braham)
Superprix – The Story of Birmingham Motor Race (Page & Collins)
Three Wheelers (Bobbitt)

See Veloce's other imprints:

A wide range of eBooks and Apps available:

www.veloce.co.uk

First published in October 2009 by Veloce Publishing Limited, Veloce House, Parkway Farm Business Park, Middle Farm Way, Poundbury, Dorchester DT1 3AR, England. Fax 01305 250479 / e-mail info@veloce.co.uk / web www.veloce.co.uk or www.velocebooks.com.
Reprinted November 2017. ISBN: 978-1-787112-64-3; UPC: 6-36847-01264-9.

Contents

Introduction

Today, many motorists tend to whine about the number of large trucks on our streets and highways. Yet, if it weren't for these multi-wheeled movers, our lives would be very different. Trucks deliver the exports and imports, move the food, manufactured goods and raw materials necessary to allow us to lead our daily lives. We can order anything, and, thanks to a truck, it will arrive a lot faster today than a century ago when horses and wagons, dirt roads, and the physical labour involved took far more time and proportionately far more money.

Trucks and roadways have improved immeasurably over the decades, and today, overnight delivery has become an expectation rather than a dream.

This "Those Were the Days ..." edition examines the American truck manufacturers and industry in the 1950s. The period began as one of great innovation, growth and prosperity for trucking, yet as the decade progressed increased market competition transformed the industry. By the end of the fifties, mergers and consolidations resulted in some of the best known names in the business disappearing or becoming nothing more than a nameplate, while a few newcomers and others survived and flourished.

Acknowledgements

There are many good people to thank in helping to publish *American Trucks of the 1950s.*

My collaborator Andrew Mort was once again essential in putting together this book. He personally handled all the images – scanning, enhancing, cropping, recording, filing and packaging, as well as accompanying me on trips shooting and collecting information.

While my son Andrew was responsible for most of the colour shots of the restored trucks, it was truck enthusiasts and collectors such as Brad Humfryes, Norman Wood, Al Gipin, Mark Hodge, Vernon Johnston, James Sercombe, C Dan Pannell, Mario Palma, George, Kevin and Charlie Tackaberry and Peter Vanderlinden, as well as GM Smith Ltd, Ford Motor Company, Chrysler Corporation and Freightliner who helped make this book come together. Special thanks go to Doug Grieve, whose personal photographic collection and knowledge of some of the rarest trucks was invaluable. Additional thanks also to Rod Grainger and his expert team at Veloce Publishing.

The 1950s would see many firms falter, whilst others, such as GMC, attempted to lead the way. (Norm Mort Collection)

Postwar prosperity

American truck manufacturers introduce new, advanced models following World War II

The demands of warfare resulted in many technological advances in trucks. Although America didn't enter the war until 1941, US plants in Europe had been converted to military production, and in 1940 orders were already being placed for half-track and 4x4 scouts, personnel cars, and special army trucks.

This circa 1923 GMC tractor was used until 1946. It is pictured moving a pleasure craft at Lake Simcoe Marine, Ontario, Canada. Following World War II there were still over 200,000 trucks on US roads which had been built prior to 1929. (James Sercombe)

International grew in size and strength with continuous improvements in its products and dealer network throughout the 1950s. The company's total sales in this decade exceeded 1.25 million units. (Andrew Mort)

Soon after VJ Day, the American truck manufacturers were ready to move toward full civilian production. Many of the trucks on American roads were close to a decade or more old, as all new trucks had been needed overseas to carry fuel and supplies to the troops. At the same time, many old tanker trucks had been laid-up during the war years due to the huge drop in domestic sales through gas rationing. With the postwar boom, the aging truck fleets needed replacement to transport materials and goods across the states.

In order to help meet the demand, the federal and state governments passed changes allowing for an

In November 1944 the War Production Board approved resumption of manufacture of the first light civilian trucks since the beginning of 1942, but it wouldn't be until December 1945 that truck and trailer rationing ended. Yet, even in 1948, companies such as Freightliner assembled their trucks using the same methods common to the prewar era. (Courtesy Freightliner)

This 1940s White is transporting a barge as part of its daily use in the early 1950s. (James Sercombe)

In 1946 over 5.5 million Americans worked in the trucking industry, and annual production rose to 951,185 units with nearly 6 million registrations. Still, the trucking industry in the US was not able to reach its full potential due to a coal strike limiting steel production, and other labour problems, such as slowdowns and shutdowns. Lack of other raw materials, such as magnesium, aluminum and rubber (for tyres), also hampered production. (Doug Grieve Collection)

This circa 1939 Leyland diesel was eventually scrapped in the 1950s, but is pictured here in the late 1940s hard at work hauling transformers on a solid rubber tyre float. (James Sercombe)

increase in the weight and length limits of trucks. Yet immediately following the war, like the auto industry, the truck manufacturers of 1946 simply resumed commercial production of warmed-over 1942 designs. At the same time, most of these older designs had been introduced since 1940, and had benefited from the requirements of the military.

Following the war, sales were brisk to oil companies, dairies and others who required large fleets. In 1947, five of America's largest fleets exceeded 6000 units, the largest owned by American Telephone and Telegraph (AT&T).

It wasn't until 1948 that totally new trucks were built. The styling was far more practical, with streamlined, art deco appearance – as seen in the late 1930s – a thing of the past. Gone, too, was the added trim and brightwork, which would diminish even further with the onset of the 1950 to 1953 Korean conflict.

Progress made in the 1940s included the fitting of safety glass. Innovative improvements consisted of more common use of a third axle for increased payload, while better weight distribution reduced cost. Lightweight semi-trailers were introduced, with the frame and body constructed from high-tensile steel, as well as

Increased driver comfort, convenience and safety were evident in the newest designs to emerge in the late 1940s. Visibility, improved cab ergonomics and hydraulic seats were also some of the latest features. (Note as well, the sleeping accommodation built into the front of the trailer which ultimately became a standard feature found in cab designs.) At the same time body and trailer manufacturers began prefabricating and standardising parts. (Doug Grieve Collection)

a demountable container and stainless steel trailers. Engines with increased torque and horsepower, and more diesel options, were now being offered, as was a full range of heavy-duty trucks. In turn, developments were made in the areas of braking, suspension, handling and steering. There was also a greater focus on driver comfort and convenience.

Countless other innovations were introduced during the 1940s, some being adopted by the entire industry, while others were further upgrades improved upon over the decade. All were to improve load capacity, and efficiency in time, expense, or both.

Soon radios were becoming standard equipment for dispatching. Tank trucks were now fitted with electrically rewound hose reels, and by 1949 warranties on tank trucks were offered against leaks, along with payment for delays resulting from repairs.

Due to the dependency on trucks covering the vast

The capabilities and advantages of six-wheel trucks were proven during the war years, and they became popular as dump trucks, as well as highway tractor units. As road weight and length restrictions increased, so did the use of these units. A further advantage over and above an increase in cargo capacity was a saving in labour costs due to fewer drivers and a move to smaller fleets. (Doug Grieve Collection)

Future trucking giant Kenworth became a division of the Pacific Car and Foundry Company in 1944. Kenworth built its first COE model 520 design in 1936. After putting a sleeper in the nose of the trailer proved unsatisfactory, a separate sleeper box was developed. The Kenworth COE pictured here is an early 1946 model based on the prewar 'Bubblenose' design. (Doug Grieve Collection)

distances in North America, they became a national priority.

In 1940, 75,000 miles of roadways (120,698km) had been identified as strategic, and President Roosevelt signed the Federal Aid Bill for highway improvements.

Although highways and turnpikes, such as the one in Pennsylvania (1940), were being constructed at state level, and road and highway construction had been a priority, it wouldn't be until 1956 that the federal government instigated plans for a highway system across the United States. As well as for the transportation of goods, the US government felt a continental highway system was imperative to national defense.

The world's first superhighways were the German autobahns of the 1930s, and General Dwight D Eisenhower was quick to realize the value of such a road system during his military campaign in World War II.

Eventually, on June 29, 1956, Eisenhower – now

In 1949 International's popular KB series was replaced by the new L series, yet production continued into the 1950s because of demand. This KB14 was the largest model available in 1949. (Andrew Mort)

This is part of a GMC advertisement that appeared in US publications across the United States in 1956, depicting the company's role in "… the great highway and waterway construction program." It was, of course, referring to the June 1956 Federal Aid Highway Act, which authorised the construction of an interstate highway system in the United States. (Norm Mort Collection)

This is the truck
that's building builders

IN the great highway and waterway construction program—in the earth-moving, bridge and dam projects—contractors are making unusual strides with a great new tool.

It's the GMC concept of a super-truck that's specially built to wrap up jobs faster and more economically.

In many models, these Blue Chip GMC's are hauling bigger payloads. Their new framing and axles, compact cabs and absence of weighty "fat" in the chassis see to it.

They're moving faster. GMC's advanced engine designs—gasoline and Diesel—pack up to 230 horsepower to provide the hustling pace contractors need.

They're making more trips. GMC's Hydra-Matic Drive* takes them out of pits in one easy sweep—ends all shifting lags in traffic—makes better time from every stop light.

They're getting up to 34% better fuel mileage than comparable trucks.

They're doubling the period between overhauls—with far less down-time in between. Replacement parts, when needed, are immediately available.

And with these faster earnings and greater operating savings, their owners are building their organizations at a handsome rate.

The photo here shows an instance that's typical in the experience of GMC dealers. It shows part of the GMC Blue Chip fleet operated by Sam Braen, prominent New Jersey contractor.

Mr. Braen bought his first GMC in 1926. Today, he has 132 Blue Chip units, from pickups to giant concrete transit mixers. And he steadily is reordering to keep pace with his business.

If you, too, have a stake in America's booming construction program, we 3,000 GMC dealers are ready to equip you as no one else can do. In any truck for any purpose—light duties to heavy—there's a great GMC waiting for you!

BLUE CHIP TRUCKS GMC

Your key to Blue Chip value

President – signed the Federal Aid Highway Act, which authorized the construction of an interstate highway system. The highways would eventually be more formerly known as the Dwight D Eisenhower System of Interstate and Defense Highways. This act authorized the construction of 41,000 miles (65,981km) of quality highways to tie the nation together. Soon after, Congress voted to increase the length to 42,500 miles (68,395km), and set superhighway standards for all interstate routes. An ambitious project, the entire system was expected to be fully completed by 1975.

Initially the highway plans bypassed large urban centres in favour of intercity transportation, but this was soon identified as a flaw. The urban interstates were added to the system at the insistence of cities that relied on the delivery of goods to meet the needs of both inner city populations and commerce, as well as those of the quickly emerging suburbs.

Construction began almost immediately, but it quickly became apparent that the entire highway system would not be completed on time. Still, by 1960 more than 10,000 miles of new highway had been opened, and the building of these rural and urban interstates was proving essential for the freight transportation industry in meeting new demands.

North of the border in Canada, similar road construction was under way. Although not as extensive or ambitious as the American plan, by the 1960s highway 401 (later to be named the Macdonald-Cartier Freeway) from Montreal to Toronto and on to the outskirts of the Windsor/Detroit border was the longest super highway in North America, at more than 500 miles. It remains to this day the busiest superhighway in North America.

Total truck (and bus) construction in the US was 754,901 units in 1940. By 1950 this figure had risen to 1,124,096, and to 1,981,519 units by 1960. America was on the move, and trucks were doing the moving!

Mack emerged as a leader in the American trucking industry by the end of the 1950s, but limited profitability resulted in a complete reorganisation by the end of the decade in order to face the newest challenges of the next. (Andrew Mort)

Delivering on time

American truck companies and models of the 1950s

Autocar

Autocar was one of the earliest vehicle manufacturers in the United States, with roots dating back to 1897 and the founding of the Pittsburgh Motor Vehicle Company by brothers John and Louis Clarke. Following a move in 1899, the company changed its name to Autocar. The two Clarke brothers were responsible for many firsts in the industry, including developing the first porcelain spark plug, the first American shaft-drive vehicle, double-reduction gear drives, and the recirculating oil lube system.

In 1908 Autocar built its first truck, and after 1911 concentrated all its production on trucks.

Autocar built both COE models (U70-U90) designed with a quick removal cab, as well as a conventional line of C (gas) and DC (diesel) models. (Doug Grieve Collection)

Autocar prospered throughout the 1920s and survived the depression years, building gasoline and Cummins diesel-powered vehicles.

Throughout World War II Autocar built military trucks and equipment, and was given government authorization to build greatly needed civilian trucks as early as 1944. Following the war, Autocar resumed full truck production, and in 1946 delivered over 5320 units. Unfortunately, this initial sales boom was followed by an industry-wide slowdown in the early 1950s.

Despite the introduction of a new deluxe cab, by 1953, with million dollar losses mounting, Autocar was taken over by the White Motor Corporation, and from then on concentrated mainly on heavy-duty,

high-powered trucks for specialised heavy hauling. Autocar's were the top-of-the-line models, and its newer deluxe cabs were utilised within the organisation on White and later Diamond T trucks.

In the 1950s, Autocar introduced its concept of 'custom engineering' and was promoted as being the 'World's Finest.' Trucks were built to meet individual customers' requirements. Due to the demand for larger and heavier vehicles, Autocar developed its AP series of on-off highway trucks. The largest was the 600hp, V12 diesel engine AP40, capable of hauling a payload capacity of 40-tons (36,280kg) with a substantially larger gross combined weight (GCW).

Autocar 1950 conventional diesel was designated C90D. While the gasoline-powered model wore an Autocar nameplate on the side of its hood, all diesel-powered models bore an Autocar diesel badge. (Andrew Mort)

The Autocar A series (A10264 model shown) featured a light aluminum chassis in 1958. This weight-saving chassis design helped increase the payload by more than 2-tons. (Doug Grieve Collection)

Powered by a 600hp V12, the AP40 was one of Autocar's largest trucks. This giant was capable of hauling 40-tons (36,280kg). (Doug Grieve Collection)

The Autocar model C65 and C90 trucks were powered by a White 490 series gasoline engine, and featured custom-built, lighter and stronger stainless steel cabs, as did the C180 and C220 Cummins diesel-powered versions. The DC75 is shown here. (Doug Grieve Collection)

Biederman – to 1956

Biederman Motors Company was established in 1920 in Cincinnati, Ohio. The company prospered, and, throughout the 1930s supplied fire departments and the military with 3-, 4- and 5-ton (2721, 3628 and 4536kg) vehicles in 4x2 tractor form, as well as a 6x6. Gas, diesel and oil driven proprietary engines were fitted during this period.

Following the war, Biederman introduced its National Standard (NS) range, powered by Hercules gas engines in four- and six-wheel guises. The slowdown in the market in the early 1950s resulted in the gradual collapse of sales, which amounted to a few dozen, and ended in 1956 when the small factory became Cincinnati's largest Chevrolet-Oldsmobile dealership.

Biederman introduced its 4- and 6-wheel NS range featuring Hercules engines and Timken axles in peacetime.
(Doug Grieve Collection)

Brockway

The origins of New York State-based Brockway date back to 1912 with the introduction of a 3-cylinder high wheeler. In 1928, with the purchase of the Indiana Truck Corporation, Brockway expanded its market from coast-to-coast and into Europe, yet the deepening depression forced Brockway to sell the Indiana concern to survive. Throughout, proprietary engines, including electric motors, were always fitted.

During World War II Brockway built large military trucks, and, in peacetime, introduced the 260 series powered by Continental ohv gas engines. All Brockway trucks from this era were powered by Continental engines and equipped with Fuller

Brockway introduced its model 258 Huskie line in 1958. This 1958 diesel example has been fully restored. Note the painted radiator shell. (Andrew Mort)

By the early 1950s Brockway was offering twenty models, from the 88 to the prewar 260 series ranging in size from 1-ton (907kg) to 30-tons (27,220kg), but sales fell to just 1752 units in 1952, and a mere 611 by 1954. This is a 1951 series 200 model. (Doug Grieve Collection)

transmissions, a two-speed Eaton axle and Timken axles.

Brockway became a division of Mack in 1956, but continued to design its own range under the 'Huskie' nameplate, which appeared in 1958. Brockway production continued until 1977 when the plant was shutdown by Mack.

Brown – to 1953

The shortlived Brown trucks of Horton Motor Lines, Charlotte, North Carolina were developed by J L Brown of the subsidiary Brown Truck and Trailer Manufacturing Company. Originally built exclusively for Horton in the prewar era, the Brown 513 introduced in 1948 was offered for general purchase,

Another first year production Brockway Huskie, but this example was gas-powered. Note the chrome radiator shell.
(Andrew Mort)

and powered by a Continental or Buda engine in a Parish frame with a Fuller transmission. By 1949 a Cummins diesel was offered. A close association with Corbitt trucks established during the war years resulted in Brown badges adorning that firm's trucks, and the sharing of cabs. Brown trucks were of high quality, but expensive and heavy. A cab-over-engine (COE) design was introduced in 1952, referred to by drivers as the 'flying saucer.' Once again, market competition and a drop in demand in the early part of the decade resulted in production ending by 1953.

Brown introduced a stylish series of COE designs in 1952-53 before halting all production. (Doug Grieve Collection)

Chevrolet & GMC
Chevrolet

Chevrolet trucks appeared in 1918, and in its first full year of peacetime production in 1919, the GM division produced 7300 units. Chevrolet trucks proved to be very popular over the ensuing decades and a full range of models were developed.

From Chevrolet, this once hard-working 1956 6400 flatbed hauler is now fully restored for show purposes only. Note the absence of chrome. (Andrew Mort)

Initially, production of the prewar models resumed, but in mid-1947 the all-new Advanced Design series was introduced, ranging from ½-ton to 2-tons (454kg to 1814kg), which included a 1½-ton COE with the larger models being powered by a 105hp, 235in³ six. Chevrolet dubbed its new cabs 'Unisteel;' they followed the industry trend toward larger, more comfortable interiors. Another redesign and styling change took place in 1954, when two forward-control Dubl-Duti chassis were unveiled.

Yet another restyling took place in 1956, featuring a wrap-around windscreen, but the big news was under the hood. The 145hp V8 Taskmaster engine was offered in the 2-ton trucks. Also new, later in '56, was the uprating to 2½-tons (2268kg) and optional power steering, and a 6-speed automatic transmission. 1957 saw the bigger trucks powered by a 205hp V8 with an all-synchromesh 5-speed transmission and optional air/hydraulic brakes. Dual headlamps, full air brakes and larger V8 engines were offered in 1958 and again in 1959.

In 1958 Chevrolet extended its truck styling cues throughout the line, from its smallest pickups to its largest trucks, such as this 100 Spartan. (Doug Grieve Collection)

GMC

General Motors Truck Company was established in 1911, and, by the time the auto show took place in 1912, the make had become officially known as GMC.

While GMC tended to borrow many of its parts from other divisions, it was a separate entity that focused solely on designing and building a full range of trucks in volume.

While GMC borrowed much of its engineering from other GM subsidiaries, it was, nevertheless, a separate division. Featured here is a 1954 GMC 660. (Andrew Mort)

During World War II, GMC built over 580,000 military vehicles, and in peacetime again offered a full line of trucks. Three new medium-duty COE models were introduced in 1948, and more followed. At the start of 1950 new and improved models were introduced in a truck line-up ranging from 1- to 20-tons (454kg to 18,140kg), with more new models added throughout the year. GMC continued to offer lightweight models without front brakes for the west coast. By 1951, GMC had introduced its 953 diesel highway tractor with a GCW of 35-tons (31,755kg).

For 1950 GMC introduced the new six-wheel HCW gas and HDCR diesel models, two new highway series tractors – the 640 and 650 – and its 275hp, 110 diesel engine (110in³/cylinder), which helped the company set a new civilian truck production record of over 100,000 units that year. (Doug Crieve Collection)

GMC also had a long history of building COE designs, such as this 1954 model. (Doug Grieve Collection)

By 1952, GMC's reliable 4-71 and 6-71 diesel engines were being dubbed 'Million Milers,' and formed the basis of a new 3-cylinder diesel fitted in its new line of medium-duty conventional trucks.

Additional models, engines and mechanical innovations continued over the next two years, but in 1955 GMC introduced its new 'Blue Chip' designs which consisted of 128 models – double the 1954 line-up with a fresh-look and over 500 significant design improvements, as well as two more V8 engines.

Automatic transmissions gained in popularity and tubeless tyres became standard in 1956, while air suspension was introduced in 1957.

As the decade drew to a close, GMC announced a line of V6 engines and a V12 that would appear in its completely new 1960 model range.

GMC's COE 1955 BBC (bumper to back of cab) models incorporated the best of both a conventional and COE design. (Doug Grieve Collection)

By 1958, highly successful GMC was marketing a line of trucks ranging from ½-ton (454kg) to 45-tons (40,815kg), and had captured over seven per cent of the total truck market. This 1958 GMC V8-powered 980 series dump truck was fully restored. (Andrew Mort)

Cook Brothers – to 1958

Whereas many truck manufacturers discovered the marketplace was shrinking quickly in the early 1950s, the Cook Brothers Equipment Company of Los Angeles, California prospered during that period, only to be absorbed by another company later in the decade and become Challenge-Cook, before disappearing completely as a nameplate in 1964.

The Cook Brothers Equipment Company focused on large 8x8 and heavy-duty trucks for the military and construction sectors, but also built on-road, one-man and offset cabs. Known as C-B, or Cook Brothers, the company's trucks utilised REO components and engines, as well as Cummins diesel engines and Ford V8s. Built to west coast specifications, the company's construction industry connections led to cement mixer manufacturer Challenger taking control in 1958. (Doug Grieve Collection)

Corbitt – to 1954 (1952)

The Corbitt Automobile Company was founded in 1907 in Henderson, North Carolina, but by 1915 was building commercial vehicles and by the mid-1920s had changed its name to the Corbitt Motor Truck

After a long production history of over forty years, Corbitt trucks fell by the wayside like so many others in the early 1950s. (Doug Grieve Collection)

Company. In the 1930s Corbitt began building large military trucks, which it continued to do throughout World War II along with a handful of civilian trucks. Known as the Corbitt Company following the war, it built conventional 6x2 and 6x4 road tractors powered by Continental gas or Cummins diesel engines, before ceasing operations in 1952. The name was revived in 1957 and built 'special order' tractors, but closed the following year.

Diamond T

Diamond T trucks date back to 1911 and soon expanded its model range as it established a name for quality and reliability.

In 1940 it became the first trucking company to introduce a 100,000 mile (160,000km) or one year guarantee on all its trucks. Like most firms, Diamond T initially carried over production of its 1942 line following the war. Late in 1949 the company

Often referred to as the Rolls-Royce of the American trucking industry, Diamond T had an enviable reputation. Seen here is a model 622 model powered by a new 150hp, 363in³ ohv engine. (Doug Grieve Collection)

DIAMOND T DIESEL 921D SERIES

"Custom-Built" to Match the Job, with a choice of

"F" Series Six-Wheeler Illustrated

+ Five Diesel Engines, ranging from 190 to 280 horsepower
+ Five 10- and 12-Speed Transmissions and Many 15-Speed Combinations
+ Four Series of Rear Axles and Ten Models of Tandem Axles
+ Three Front Axle Positions to meet varied Legal Restrictions

Max. Gross Vehicle Weight . . . 30-41,000 lbs.; Six-Wheelers . . . 41-70,000 lbs.
Maximum Gross Combination Weight (including Six-Wheelers) . . . 68-120,000 lbs.

LIGHT-WEIGHT COMPANION 922D SERIES

Duplicates design, construction, capacity and options of 921D Series, but with weight reduced by use of aluminum and other light-weight options. Specifications of 922D Series models include Alloy Steel frame, heat-treated, 10"x3½"x¼", Aluminum Front Bumper, Aluminum and Lightweight Crossmembers and Light-weight tank supports, Aluminum Battery box, Hopkins Muffler and Light-weight Stack, Rod type Radiator Braces, B-W Spring Type Emergency Brake for six-wheelers. Aluminum fuel tanks can be supplied in a range of sizes and types and aluminum hoods are available for both Basic and "F" Models.

Diamond T introduced another all-new, heavy-duty line for 1951 consisting of the model 660, 720 and 722, and a Cummins diesel-powered 921. (Doug Grieve Collection)

The Diamond T tilt-cab 921 C diesel featured a 68,000 gross weight. This particular example was used for the Midnight Chief Run, a tight 24-hour run between Akron, Ohio to Cleveland and Minneapolis-St Paul for the shipping company Motor Cargo. (Doug Grieve Collection)

By 1953 the Diamond T line had been expanded further to include the model 950 and 951. These bigger trucks were powered by a 300hp Cummins diesel or a 280hp Buda diesel (model 950 shown). (Doug Grieve Collection)

Diamond T diesels meter the minutes for Motor Cargo's "Midnight Chief"

The 1953 National Design Award was a trucking industry first, given to Diamond T for its COE model featuring a counterbalancing system and unique vent window design that was eventually adopted by virtually the entire trucking industry. This cab was used by both International and Hendrickson for twenty years until 1972. Diamond T used the COE design initially on its model 422, 522 and 622 trucks. (Doug Grieve Collection)

introduced its first all-new postwar models – the 1½- to 5-ton (1367-4535kg) Super Service 420, 520 and 620, and later 322 Diamond Ts.

Like many other firms, Diamond T utilised International's 'Comfort Cab' by 1951, yet would win a National Design Award for its own tilt-cab COE in 1953. This award was an industry first, and given due to its counterbalancing system and unique vent window design that was adopted by virtually the entire trucking industry.

Although the company had continued to prosper – in part to military contracts – the changing times resulted in Diamond T abandoning the light truck market and focusing on trucks weighing 3-tons (2722kg) and more.

White bought Diamond T in 1958, and production of both Diamond T and previously purchased REO was moved to Lancing, Michigan in 1960. The 1959 Diamond Ts were built utilising the Autocar D cab first seen in 1950. Also in that year, production commenced of the new Diamond T 5000 series.

Dodge

The Dodge brothers began building trucks in Detroit in 1916. The company was purchased by Walter P Chrysler in 1927 to become the Dodge Division of Chrysler Corporation. The firm built over 500,000 military trucks from 1943-1945. In 1947, Dodge had its best year ever, and its biggest truck was the

In 1951 Dodge introduced a new, fuller line of freshly styled trucks, including the 4- and 5-ton (3628kg and 4535kg) T, V and Y series. These trucks featured air brakes and the choice of a 145hp or 151hp gas engine. (Doug Grieve Collection)

In 1956 Dodge surprised the industry by fitting only V8 engines in all its COE models. The HM8 had a GCW of 30,000lb and came in three wheelbase sizes – 108, 132 and 152 inches. (Doug Grieve Collection)

Dodge introduced a new tandem line of trucks in 1957 which was restyled in 1958. This 1958 brochure extolled the virtues of the latest design innovations.
(Doug Grieve Collection)

Dodge and Fargo in the 1950s were very much like Ford, Mercury, GMC and Chevrolet, in that they differed only slightly in model line-up, nameplates, and trim, and were often sold only in specific countries and markets. Fargo offered an H model (17,000lb maximum GVW) and a K model (21,000lb maximum GVW), as this page from the 1956 brochure on the Fargo K8 notes.
(Norm Mort Collection)

series WK 3-ton (2722kg). For 1948 Dodge restyled its trucks, and its largest was a 4-ton (3628kg) capacity powered by a 377in^3 six. With the start of the Korean conflict, Dodge focused once more on military vehicles, but in 1951 it introduced a new, expanded line of freshly styled trucks including the 4- and 5-ton (328 and 4535kg) T, V and Y series. The smaller 2½-ton (2268kg) series J trucks featured a COE design in 1953, and claimed the shortest turning radius in the industry at 37½ft (11m).

Chrysler's 331in^3 Hemi V8 engine became available on some models in 1954, and in the entire truck line by 1955, before this engine ended production at the end of 1959.

1957 saw a new tandem line of trucks unveiled, yet these were restyled in 1958. The largest Dodge trucks in 1959 were the D-900 and T-900 powered by the 234hp Hemi V8.

DeSoto
Dodge also exported trucks to Great Britain during the 1950s, but these bore the DeSoto or Fargo badge, and were sold through outlets other than Dodge dealers.

RUGGED AND COMPACT! CAB-OVER-ENGINE MODELS WITH V-8 ENGINES

Famous for easy handling, these great new Fargo trucks combine minimum length with maximum manoeuvrability plus the same outstanding engineering and solid construction as conventional models. Shorter wheelbase is required to accommodate a given-length body. Over-all truck length is also reduced.

SPECIFICATIONS

	Model HM	Model KM	Model HHM
Max. G.V.W.	17,000 lbs.	21,000 lbs.	18,000 lbs.
Max. G.C.W.	30,000 lbs.	45,000 lbs.	35,000 lbs.
Max. body and payload allowance (approx.)	11,950 lbs.	15,000 lbs.	12,800 lbs.
Cab-and-chassis	12,125 lbs.	15,125 lbs.	13,100 lbs.
Wheelbase, inches	108, 132, 162	108, 120, 132, 162	108, 132, 162
9' stake body	11,350 lbs.		12,325 lbs.
ENGINE:	**V-8**	**V-8**	**V-8**
Displacement	269.6 cu. in.	331.1 cu. in.	269.6 cu. in.
Max. gross horsepower	172	201	172
Max. gross torque	262 lb.-ft.	311 lb.-ft.	262 lb.-ft.

In 1956, Fargo also offered the K and H models in a COE design known as a model HM (17,000lb), an HMM (18,000lb), and a KM (21,000lb). (Norm Mort Collection)

The new postwar Fageol sold in very small numbers, and very few survive today. (Doug Grieve Collection)

The once-proud Fageol nameplate was revived in 1950 with a line-up of vans such as this one. (Doug Grieve Collection)

Fargo

Fargo trucks were introduced by Chrysler in 1928 as its Fleet Sales organisation, and used in Canada and for Canadian exports around the world. Fargo models were identical to Dodge trucks except for nameplates and minor trim.

Fageol – to 1954

Fageol was a well known truck manufacturer dating back to 1916, but it failed to survive the Depression. In 1950 the Twin Coach Co. of Kent, Ohio, which had also been founded by the Fageol brothers, revived the marque to build the Fageol Super Freighter and a smaller delivery vehicle known as the Pony Express. The Super Freighter began life as a line of removal vans based on old, converted Fruehauf stainless steel semi-trailers, but in 1951 custom-built versions appeared based on new Freuhauf components in both four- and six- wheeled versions, powered by IHC engines. The Pony Express had lasted a short time only, while the entire venture ceased production in 1954.

Federal

Federal was established in 1910 in Detroit, Michigan, and by 1913 had built over 1000 units. The company flourished over the decades, and during World War II received four citations for its contributions of military vehicles and high production numbers.

Immediately following the war, upgraded prewar designs were offered, but in 1951 Federal introduced its Style Liner 1800 model powered by a 145hp engine of the company's own design. The Style Liner featured hypoid gear single-speed or double-reduction drive axles. Ten more models followed,

along with additional variations, all powered by either diesel or gasoline engines.

In 1952 Federal's truck division became part of Federal Fawick Corporation, but, following losses, Federal was purchased in 1955 by NAPCO Industries of Minneapolis, Minnesota, which specialised in fitting 4x4 drivelines on Chevrolet, GMC and other manufacturers' trucks. With production relocated, Federal began building only special order trucks, some received from the USAF and other US military forces. In 1959 Federal abandoned truck production following an order solely to supply axles for military trucks.

Introduced in 1951, the conventional, heavy-duty Federal Stye Liner trucks featured hypoid gear axles and radius-rod drive as standard equipment. Optional equipment included double reduction axles. This is a 1953 version (Doug Grieve Collection)

Ford

In 1917 Ford announced the production of the first factory-built model TT, offering a heavy-duty frame and longer wheelbase for greater strength and flexibility, a stiffer rear suspension with special tyres and wheels to handle heavy payloads, and a sturdier rear axle for tough hauling.

By 1923 over 225,000 Ford trucks had been built

Ford entered the 1950s with a total of 175 different truck models. Pictured here is a 1952 V8-powered F8 Big Job. The 317in³ Cargo King V8 was an overhead valve Y-block engine rated at 155hp. (Andrew Mort)

in North America, and by 1924 Ford was delivering factory fitted, all-steel truck bodywork with an open pickup-type box on the model TT chassis in three styles. Ford trucks were offered in everything from light-duty panel deliveries to stake bodies, dumpers, tank trucks, and even fire engines. The new model BB Ford trucks in 1932 highlighted the introduction of V8 power, parallel semi-elliptic rear springs, and

1953 was Ford's golden anniversary year, celebrated with new ideas and new model designations. The industry sales-leading Ford ZF-800 was one of the trucks that dominated the roads in the 1950s. Pictured here is a 1953 Big Job 800 highway tractor. (Andrew Mort)

enlarged fuel tanks repositioned below the seat for greater safety.

The return of the in-between 'One Tonner' pickup, and Ford's first COE in 1938, put Ford at the forefront of model availability. By 1942 Ford trucks were offered in 126 separate body chassis combinations, including conventional and cab-over models, a choice of three engines – a four, six, or eight – four wheelbases, and ½-, ¾-, 1- and 1½-ton (454, 605, 907 and 1361kg) payload ratings.

Ford's all-new postwar 1948 Bonus Built trucks were offered in 139 variations and now known as the F series. The F-7 and F-8 Big Job models brought Ford into the heavy truck field. Ford trucks were offered

in 164 models for 1949, and 175 by 1950, with the introduction of the larger F-5 Parcel Van.

In this highly competitive postwar era, every year brought upgrades and styling changes. The

Ford's Triple Economy Trucks, series F-750, F-800, and F-900, boasted of new power, comfort, styling and safety. (Norm Mort Collection)

Vernor's Ginger Ale – one of the oldest soft drinks in America – was very popular in the 1950s, and unique in flavour, as it was aged in wooden kegs. Here we see one of the company's fleet of Ford F8s in 1953, in front of the factory, which is painted like a castle with the company's trademark. A gnome-like character looks on. (Ford Motor Company)

all-new Economy Truck line for 1953 featured new 'Driverized' cabs featuring more comfort and convenience. The Economy Truck line also featured set-back front axles and wider tracks, which translated into an increase in front overhangs for greater stability and easier manoeuvering.

In 1953 Ford became one of the first truck manufacturers to introduce an optional automatic transmission. Additional highlights of 1953's new designs included the availability of direct drive and overdrive, and fully synchronized 5-speed gearboxes for the 194 models offered.

Ford's 1959 brochures touted the comfort, roominess, visibility, and accessibility for maintenance of its COE tilt-cab C series. Ford's new company sales slogan was "Go Fordward For Savings in 1959." (Norm Mort Collection)

As the decade closed, Ford's popular C tilt-cab and tandem axle T series, along with its conventional F series line-up, put the company in a very strong position to face the even greater changes and difficult challenges that were coming in the 1960s. (Norm Mort Collection)

The most important trucking news of the year!

MERCURY TRUCKS

announce for 1951

1 The greatest line of Mercury Trucks in history!

Over 80 Mercury Truck models from which to choose exactly the right truck for your work. Complete range from ½ to 5 tons.

2 Mercury's improved "Loadomatic" economy!

An engineering accomplishment that automatically adjusts timing and gasoline flow to match changing speed, load and power requirements.

The 1951 Mercury Truck line is designed to offer exactly the right truck for your job. Three great Mercury Truck engines, 9 series, 12 wheelbases. Optional axle ratios, 2-speed axles and many other features. Call in at your Mercury Truck Dealer today. See the complete line of new models, the many new features . . . and select the right truck for *your* job!

Mercury Trucks' "Loadomatic" synchronizes carburetor, distributor action. It gets the *most* power from the *least* gasoline . . . automatically meters and fires the right amount of gas at the right instant regardless of changing speed, load, and power requirements. "Loadomatic" saves money . . . gives better engine performance under all conditions. On all models from ½ to 5 tons.

Three Great Engines —All engines are V-type 8-cylinder! Up to 145 horsepower. Designed with plenty of reserve power—move loads with ease and economy.

Custom and Standard Cabs — Custom Cab has sponge rubber seat cushion, sound-proofing, special upholstery and trim, twin horns and many other features.

Steering Column Gearshift — Another new feature on the light Mercury M-1 ½-ton models. Extra convenience, additional room, greater comfort.

New Front-End Styling —New and improved front-end styling. A wider, massive, more distinctive appearance of strength and ruggedness.

Mercury Truck Catalogue —"How to select the right truck for your job" also contains every detail of the new 1951 Mercury Trucks. Get a copy today.

Move it with MERCURY for less!
T R U C K S

SEE YOUR MERCURY TRUCK DEALER

In Canada, the Ford Motor Company offered a full line of Mercury trucks, as well as its Ford models. The Mercury vehicles were sold through a different dealer network, and differed slightly in appearance, fittings and options. (Norm Mort Collection)

Ford's truck designations were completely revised for 1953. The conventional models became known as the F-100, F-350 in pickup form, and so on up to the new Ford Super Truck, the F-900, while the parcel vans became the P series and the COE models became the S series.

In 1954 the ZF-800 became the sales leader in its class, while the standard, beefed-up, Power King V8s gave the rest of the '54 Ford truck fleet an all-ohv engine line-up.

Ford expanded further into the heavy-truck field with its new T series tandem – or dual axle models – with the 10-wheeler conventional, and went on to claim 30 per cent of the truck market in 1955 with record sales.

In 1957 the new C series COE was introduced with its cab hinged at the front to tilt forward for drivetrain access. This design would continue in concept right into the 1990s and be copied by many in the industry.

By 1959 truck model choices had been expanded to 370, which included the arrival of the first factory-built four-wheel-drive vehicles.

Freightliner

Leland James founded Freightliner Corporation in Salt Lake City on August 19th, 1942. Having been a trucker from the age of 19, he had already established Consolidated Freightways in 1929. Now, he was looking for a truck that was more durable, lighter, had a better ride, and a higher payload to help increase profits. James hadn't planned on entering the truck manufacturing business, but there seemed little interest amongst established makers to build a lightweight aluminium COE design.

James had convinced ten other western-based freight carriers to join him in forming Consolidated Freightways Inc. to serve a total of ten states. Early in 1940 this group also established a subsidiary known as Freightways Manufacturing Company Inc.

Salt Lake City was a central location and a source of cheap labour, and thus a small garage was established to build ten pilot truck models. The idea was to prove to established truck manufacturers that a lightweight COE was a practical design. During this time aluminum trailers were also built.

Over the next eight years those first ten trucks each racked-up over 750,000 miles of service. Three series of COEs were built with each evolving in its own way, but they all had heat-treated alloy steel frames and aluminum cab skins.

James decided to send the proprietary pieces unique to the Freightway trucks to a manufacturer, but when the workmanship turned out to be inferior, Freightliner entered the truck manufacturing business.

When America entered the war in 1941, the government seized all aluminum and magnesium supplies and Freightways took on war projects. At the same time, the US government charged the company with operating a monopoly. Freightliner had grown to the point where it served all 48 states and three Canadian provinces. As a consequence, Freightliner and its affiliated carriers accepted a consent decree that broke up the arrangement.

On January 2 1947, James re-opened Freightliner with no factory, no materials and no money, but was joined by members of the original group to rebuild Freightliner.

Freightliner resumed building an all-aluminum COE, and, thanks to the war, aluminum and magnesium alloys had improved greatly. As a result, the lighter alloys would be found in the frame rails, axle housings, cabs, brake drums, crossmembers, radiators, etc – and even in such small parts as license plate hangers and floor pedals.

Starting all over again, Freightliner built a plant in Portland that opened in September 1947. Freightliner did have one thing in its favour at this point – a proven record for building a dependable truck. In 1948, Freightliner built its first all-aluminum cab. (Courtesy Freightliner)

Leland James modernised the CF fleet by converting to the modern COE 800 Bubblenose design in 1950. As a result, in 1950, Freightliner sold its first truck to the Hyster Company of Portland, the first customer not affiliated with CF. The order was for an 800 with a built-in sleeper. This made it the first transcontinental COE tractor with an integral sleeper. The Bubblenose 800 established Freightliner's legitimacy as a truck manufacturer, and set new standards in the industry. As a result, production rose to three trucks a week in 1950. (Courtesy Freightliner)

In 1953, Freightliner built two new models. The Cummins diesel-powered, WF-4864 Spacemaker COE, 48in cab and four-wheel tractor was designed with an extremely short wheelbase for pulling double trailers. (Courtesy Freightliner)

Thirty Freightliners were built, along with some trailer production, service work, and the selling of parts; as a result the company was able to afford to design the next generation Freightliner.

Known as the Bubblenose, or model 800, it featured an enlarged, aluminum radiator, and to increase interior space the bubble of the cab nose rose up to the windscreen. The 800 set new standards in the industry, and was the lightest truck on the road. It soon established Freightliner's legitimacy as a truck manufacturer, which resulted in Freightliner production being moved to an assembly line. By 1950 three trucks a week were being built.

In 1951 America's oldest truck manufacturer signed an agreement with the youngest.

White-Freightliner would be sold and serviced through White dealers, which allowed Freightliner to concentrate on design and production. Over the next 25 years, Freightliner would sell over 100,000 trucks through White dealers in the US and Canada.

A new Portland, Oregon plant opened in 1952, with longtime Freightliner partner Ken Self designing a production system flexible enough to cope with any customer's special needs. While production in the first year in 1950 reached 251 units, by 1956 this had more than doubled.

In the latter half of 1958, the industry's first full 90 degree, tilt-cab COE was introduced; sales increased a further 33 per cent, and would continued to expand into the 1960s.

Also appearing in 1953 was Freightliner's shift-on-the-fly, four-wheel, 4x4 WF-5844T, which helped pioneer the use of doubles, thanks to its superior pulling power and traction. (Courtesy Freightliner)

One of the most interesting FWD models to appear in the 1950s was the BXU, or Blue Ox. It was offered in 4x4, 6x6, 10x8 and also 12x10 configuration. (Doug Grieve Collection)

FWD

FWD takes its name from its original 1910 car and truck design, Four Wheel Drive. The FWD Automobile Company was officially founded in Clintonville, Wisconsin in 1912. World War I resulted in a flood of orders, to the extent that FWD licensed other manufacturers to help build the 15,000 3- and 5-ton (2722 and 4535kg) trucks required.

Surviving the 1930s, FWD built trucks for the military once again.

The late 1940s saw the introduction of new light duty and heavy-duty conventional cab and COE models. The heavy-duty U series was popular, with a gross weight capacity of up to 22-tons (19,954kg). Conventional cab design during the 1950s followed the industry norm with some widened COE.

Hayes

The Canadian Hayes trucks were originally known as Hayes-Anderson and Hayes-Lawrence. The Vancouver-based concern was established in 1928, with the company focused on conversions and building trucks for the logging industry and dock work.

Re-organised in 1934, Hayes went on to become a dealer for Leyland, and began utilising those engines and components in its own trucks.

Following World War II, Hayes introduced a new line of highway tractors powered by Detroit diesel, Leyland, Cummins, Caterpillar – and even Rolls-Royce engines. This specialised production was on a small scale. In 1969 Mack became a major stockholder, and the nameplate eventually disappeared in 1975.

In 1951, Hayes had an advertisement in *Motor* magazine in which it pointed out that its 29-35 model could carry enough logs to build five houses – each with five rooms – in part thanks to a huge, purpose-built Carter radiator. (Norm Mort Collection)

Hendrickson began to specialise in low profile cab-over and cab-forward crane-carriers fitted with tandem or tri-axles front and rear, capable of a 200-ton capacity. Another interesting design to emerge in the 1950s was this one-man cab. (Doug Grieve Collection)

Hendrickson

After being in the truck building business since 1900, Magnus Hendrickson and his sons established their own Hendrickson Motor Truck Company in 1913. As well as achieving success with its own truck designs, Hendrickson built International fire trucks in the 1930s. By 1941, Hendrickson was building both Waukesha gas and diesel Cummins-powered trucks, covering capacities of up to 10-tons (9070kg).

In 1948, the Mobile Equipment Division took over the building of conventional Hendrickson trucks utilising International K series cabs. In 1950, when the Hendrickson B series appeared, these models also used the various International cabs available. This series was soon followed by a new COE, but featured a Hendrickson rear tilting cab and hood, as well as an International CO-405 cab. Other manufacturer's cabs were utilised in the 1950s, and Hendrickson began to specialise in crane-carrier

production, low-profile fuel tankers, snow clearance vehicles, scissor lift, cargo handling trucks for airport use, and super-heavyweight trucks for 200-tons (181,400kg) and more. The chassis designs for these vehicles were soon being purchased by other manufacturers.

International

International Harvester has a long, proud history in building trucks, heavy equipment, tractors, etc. The

International's L series replaced the popular KB late in 1949, and featured headlamps mounted in the fenders and a one-piece, curved windscreen. The cab design was later shared with Diamond T. The diesel- and gas-powered versions were joined by LP-gas engine models in 1952. Pictured is a 1953 L160 stake truck. (Andrew Mort)

(Left) International's advertising in 1951 was not only about its trucks, but the kind of buyers that purchased its trucks. (Norm Mort Collection)

The new 1953 R series International models were fitted with all-steel, conventional cabs built by the Chicago Manufacturing Company that had evolved from the L series. International dubbed these Comfo-vision cabs, and they featured a one-piece curved windscreen with a sleeper option. (Doug Grieve Collection)

The R was eventually replaced by the Fleetstar in the mid-1960s. Although prolific in number, some models were quite rare. This 1953 RDF310 was powered by a Cummins diesel, one of just twenty-four built. (Andrew Mort)

International line began with its early 1900s high-wheelers.

The founders behind International were Cyrus H McCormick, Henry Weber and William Deering. These three men began their careers in farming equipment and wagons dating back to the mid-19th century.

Weber established a wagon works, but by the late-1890s it was apparent that the automobile was beginning to challenge the horse. McCormick and Deering had both had a hand at building a horseless carriage, and neither was impressed. In the meantime, the two men merged their respective farming equipment companies along with Weber and two others to create the International Harvester Company in 1902. Both McCormick and Deering had long associations with farmers, so it wasn't surprising

International announced the S series in 1955, which essentially replaced the much revered R models. The S series utilised many of the design components of the L and R series trucks, and was an interim model designed to maintain sales until the new golden anniversary A series. (Doug Grieve Collection)

This 1954 International 'high binder' with sleeper was fully restored for show purposes. The 'high binder' term stems from the raised cab sitting over the engine. (Andrew Mort)

the first International tractor that appeared in 1906 would be followed by its High Wheeler truck in 1907.

After the first one hundred trucks, a new plant was built in Akron, Ohio, and annual production soon rose to 1000 High Wheelers a year, which was sustained until 1916.

There was no stopping International from then, as new truck models were introduced throughout the 1920s, '30s, and into the '40s. International's first diesel was introduced in 1933. In 1944, the company introduced its now familiar red 'I' over the black 'H' badge.

In the 1950s, International was responsible for numerous innovative truck designs. The K – introduced in 1940 – had quickly become an industry legend, but in 1950 it was replaced by the more

modern L series with a choice of 87 different models. The L series then evolved into the R, which was joined by the S and CO (cab over) series in 1955. Also, there were the Emeryville DCO-405 models built in the mid-1950s, which provided International with a wide variety of models to choose from to accommodate the change in weight and length limits, and the needs of customers using the ever increasing, expanded highway system across the United States.

The line-up was further expanded with the V series, including the VCO, which appeared in 1956. A more powerful engine was also offered in the form of the Cummins diesel.

In celebration of its 50th anniversary in 1957, International introduced fresh styling and new models in its truck line. The A series, AC and ACO from 1957-59, and subsequent B and BC series in 1959, helped push International to the forefront of the industry and sell an unbelievable 1,283,000+ vehicles in that decade. That number also included school buses, military vehicles, construction vehicles, etc.

The A and subsequent B series International trucks of 1959 helped International achieve 12.7 per cent of the US truck market by 1959. When the B series was introduced in 1959 with its dual vertical headlamps, it was initially available with either the Black Diamond 6-cylinder engine or the more powerful V-266 V8. Later that year only the V-266 and larger V-304 V8 became standard in B series trucks.
(Doug Grieve Collection)

This 1953 International has the distinction of being the very first off the Canadian assembly line that year.
Fully refurbished, it is driven and enjoyed regularly by its Picton, Ontario owner. (Andrew Mort)

Throughout the 1950s, Kenworth experimented with a variety of engines and cab designs, such as this CBE, or cab-beside-engine. (Doug Grieve Collection)

Kenworth

Kenworth's roots date back to 1912 in Portland, Oregon when George and Louis Gerlinger Jr created the Gersix truck company. The name was based on the family name plus the Continental Six engine that they used. Despite claims that Gersix trucks were designed specially for the poor roads and rainy weather of the northwest, the company went into receivership in 1917. Rescue came in the form of two investors: Edgar Worthington and Frederick Keen.

With America in the war, the company built its trucks with whatever parts it could acquire. Following World War I the firm began building approximately four trucks per month. Keen retired in 1919 and sold his interest in Gersix to Harvey Kent and Edgar Worthington. Fifty-three trucks were built in 1922, and in 1923 the company was reincorporated under the name Kenworth.

By 1928 sales increased to a point that a new assembly plant was necessary. In its new location and with the onset of the Depression, Kenworth also began building trailers, and entered into bus manufacturing in 1932.

Kenworth's early 1950s 'Needle Nose' proved highly popular with western carriers.
(Doug Grieve Collection)

Also for 1950, Kenworth introduced its famous flat-nosed K series, which helped the company surpass the 1000 annual trucks total in 1952. (Doug Grieve Collection)

Still, truck development continued, and it was Kenworth that introduced the first diesel engine rig, powered by a 100hp, HA-4 Cummins. In 1933 Kenworth announced its first sleeper cab and in 1936 the company began building its own cabs following the demise of the Hieser Body Works.

During World War II Kenworth built over 2100 trucks for the military, which included more than

Kenworth introduced a COE version of its 900 series in 1957, but, rather than referring to it as a COE, it was dubbed a CSE, or cab-surrounding-engine. (Doug Grieve Collection)

1900 six-wheeled M-1 wreckers. Following the deaths of the company's owners in 1944, Pacific Car and Foundry Company purchased Kenworth.

Immediately after the war, Kenworth was forced to turn down over 2000 orders due to a lack of production capacity.

Between 1940 and 1950 Kenworth's largest customer had been the Arabian American Oil Company (ARAMCO) which ordered over 1000 units. Interestingly, at that point 40 per cent of the company's business was foreign orders.

In 1950, along with the new model 801, Kenworth built its model 853, production of which eventually totalled 1700 units exclusively for ARAMCO.

Also for 1950, Kenworth introduced its famous flat-nosed K series, helping the company surpass the 1000 annual trucks total in 1952.

An unusual cab design unveiled in 1953 was the Kenworth CBE (cab beside engine), built along with a conventional cab and a popular COE model soon nicknamed the Bullnose.

1956 saw Kenworth introduce its conventional cab 900 series trucks with a dropped frame for a shorter, lighter chassis. A full-tilt COE design followed in 1957, and, by 1959, Kenworth trucks were also being assembled in Canada and Mexico.

Throughout the 1950s Kenworth experimented with a variety of engines, including a 200lb (91kg) gas turbine engine developed in conjunction with Boeing, and 375hp air-cooled engines.

Leyland Canada – 1948-57
Although Leyland had been in Canada since 1920, following World War II the operation was completely

This late 1950s Kenworth 500 series COE model was offered with either a 73in sleeper cab or an 86in sleeper cab style. By opting for the smaller sleeper, the operator had an additional 13 inches of cargo space. (Doug Grieve Collection)

Like its previous models, the Leyland Bison also proved unsuitable in the North American market, despite claims and extensive testing. The continuously long hauls and heavy loads played havoc with its diesel engine. Parts supply and inadequate coast-to-coast service were also major factors in its failure. (Doug Grieve Collection)

The underpowered Leyland Beaver failed in the highly competitive 1950s truck market in Canada, as did the later Leyland Canada models, such as this one. (Doug Grieve Collection)

re-established and reorganized. Leyland Motors (Canada) Ltd introduced its Comet, which was criticised due to lack of power. In 1951 Leyland again failed in the marketplace with its Canadian Beaver, Bison and Bull Moose models, all powered by the company's own diesel. Another, more powerful range was introduced in 1952, but again floundered. In 1956, the Leyland-Canada range was introduced. At first this range was more successful, but the diesel engines proved unreliable at hauling heavy loads the long distances across Canada. At one point Leyland Motors had its own 300,000ft² assembly plant on 225 acres in Longueuil, Quebec, as well as a proving ground, but all this closed in 1957.

Mack

The Mack Brothers Company was established in Brooklyn, New York, in 1903, but by 1905 the firm had relocated to Allentown, Pennsylvania. It built Manhattan trucks before establishing the Mack as a brand name.

The company prospered, and the characteristic 'Bulldog' moniker was established by 1916. Tank transporters, cargo trucks and 6-ton transporters were built throughout the war years. Following World War II, Mack proceeded to focus on models with a 3-ton capacity or more, and expanded its bus line in the closing days of the 1940s.

In 1950, Mack was still building its popular and reliable L series of heavy-duty trucks, which had first appeared in 1940. Certain models in this series utilised aluminum components, especially in the long-wheelbase LTSW, which was Mack's first west coast tractor. More powerful engines of up to 360hp were also introduced by 1950.

A significant introduction was the new B series of 1953, which would go on to become one of the most successful truck lines in the company's history (127,786 built from 1946-1965). The wide array of

This is a 1958 Mack B75 3LS on display at the America on Wheels museum in Allentown, Pennsylvania. Only 476 examples of these models were built from 1955 to 1966. The B70 series, with its larger engine compartment, was fitted with the 672in³ diesel engine, which was favoured by the mid-west and west coast trucking firms. (Andrew Mort)

Introduced in 1940, the Mack L series resumed production after the war with some models being built into the 1960s.
The LJ was one of the heavier models and was replaced in 1956 by the B-70. This is a 1950 gas-powered LJ model 85.
(Andrew Mort)

models ranged from the small B-20 with a 17,000lb gross vehicle weight (GVW) to the 60,000lb GVW B-42 tractor. Larger versions would be added over the years.

Mack's success on the road was almost equalled by its success in the off-road market, as the model range also expanded in 1953 to include the new

west coast W-71S and H models. By 1954, the Mack Thermodyne diesel engine was standard in the H series, with the petrol engine optional.

In 1955 a shorter wheelbase COE D series was introduced for city transport, powered by a standard Magnadyne gas engine. Being more of a cab-forward

The Mack A series appeared in 1950, replacing the E series, and was sold in a wide range of variants over the years. Its good looks, reliability and popularity made it one of the company's most successful models, and it found a variety of admirers throughout the trucking industry. (Doug Grieve Collection)

design, it featured Mack's verti-lift cab, which lifted vertically, either manually or with optional hydraulics. The line was subsequently replaced by the N series in 1958, featuring a tilt-cab.

Mack introduced the G series ultra-short BBC truck in 1959. Its upright, short cab design still allowed for a wide variety of engines to be fitted to suit the needs of any hauler.

The Mack B series began production in 1953, although its design concepts dated back to the experimental M8 in 1945, and the cab-forward version of 1948, dubbed the M8U. The stylish B series cab featured greater room, comfort and improved ventilation, as well as a 'veed' windscreen that cut glare. The wider-at-the-front frame, combined with easily disassembled panels, made servicing easier, while the resulting wider track improved handling. B75 with factory sleeper shown. (Doug Grieve Collection)

The H series H-60T and H-61T came with an aluminum cab. This lightweight – commonly known as the 'Cherry Picker' – had the ability to haul heavy payloads, and, with its high cab and large bumper-to-back of cab measurement, could accommodate a 35ft trailer while remaining within the 45ft legal limit. In 1954, the H-62T and H-63T were introduced featuring a 1ft reduction in cab height, yet they were still over 9ft tall. This is a 1956 Mack H63T. (Andrew Mort)

The Mack D series featured a boxier-looking, cab-forward design, although it was called a COE. It had the unique verti-lift cab, which could be operated manually or ordered with an optional hydraulic lifting mechanism. The short-lived D – with its large, flat veed windscreen – was replaced in 1958 by the N series. (Doug Grieve Collection)

The 1958 N series featured a Budd-built cab used in the C series Ford, which, by spanning four decades, was one of the longest-running production trucks ever built. (Doug Grieve Collection)

The Mack long wheelbase W-71S, which made wide use of alloy and was fitted with a standard 200hp, Cummins diesel engine. It was designed to meet the axle spacing laws in effect in many of the western states in the US. All of the W models were fitted with aftermarket-only sleepers. (Doug Grieve Collection)

This 1957 Mack COE H67 sleeper saw plenty of service throughout the New England states in its day. First introduced in 1954, the H60 COE series remained in production until 1962. (Andrew Mort)

As the decade ended, Mack introduced its latest BBC G series. Its short cab length took full advantage of the greater standardisation in state GCW and overall length regulations, while incorporating greater driver comfort and ease of maintenance. (Doug Grieve Collection)

A very rare example of the handful of MacDonald trucks built in the 1950s. Never a large company, production had been very limited since the Peterbilt takeover, but, following World War II, it was down to a trickle. The last were rear-wheel-drive, the self-loader model C being one of the company's final series. (Doug Grieve Collection)

MacDonald – to 1952
In 1920 the MacDonald Truck and Tractor Company was established in San Francisco, California. Production was taken over by the Union Construction Company, then by MacDonald Truck and Manufacturing, and ultimately by Peterbilt following World War II. Production went down to a trickle with just four trucks built in 1948, and only two in 1949,

yet a few low-bed trucks were still being built through to 1952.

Oshkosh
The successful 4x4 trucking firm known as Duplex re-organised itself in 1918 to form Oshkosh Motor Truck Manufacturing Company in Oshkosh, Wisconsin.

In the late 1940s Oshkosh introduced its first

This is a rare surviving example of an Oshkosh WT2206. The W series was introduced by the company in 1953, and remained in production until 1959. Many were employed for firefighting, snow plowing or heavy construction work. (Andrew Mort)

OSHKOSH W-200 SERIES SPECIFICATIONS

- 130 HORSEPOWER AT 3000 R. P. M.

- GROSS VEHICLE WEIGHT 21,000 LBS. NOMINAL

- CHASSIS WEIGHT WITH CAB AND STANDARD EQUIPMENT 8430 LBS.

OSHKOSH

OSHKOSH MOTOR TRUCK INC.
OSHKOSH   WISCONSIN

Oshkosh – the first 50-50 series 4x4 conventional appeared in 1955, featuring a front axle set well back under the cab doors. For ready-mix cement and the construction industry, it was built with 8x8, 8x6 and 10S6 drives. Tandem front steering axles and four rear axles resulted in a 12x10 drive. Oshkosh used International curved windshield cabs from 1956 through to 1966. (Doug Grieve Collection)

6x6, while in the long running W series, the W-2800 conventional appeared featuring a set-back front axle, a transfer box with planetary gearing, a torque-proportioning differential, and a 35-ton (31,755kg) payload. Also, the new WT-2206 line appeared in 1953, designed specifically for air field snow clearance. In 1955 the 50-50 series was announced, followed in 1956 by various models utilising International cabs. In 1956 the Model 1832 became the first tandem-axle Oshkosh and featured a weight rating of 9-ton (8165kg) for the front axle and 16-ton (14,515kg) for the rear tandem.

Peterbilt

Peterbilt was based on what was once Fageol. In 1939, Alfred 'Al' Peterman, a lumber baron in the state of Washington, bought the failing Fageol truck

company for a mere fifty thousand dollars, but in 1944 the company came under the control of a group of employees. The first Peterbilt of the new decade to appear in 1950 was the model 280 and 350 COE.

The Peterbilt model 350 was offered in COE and conventional design. The COE featured swing-out fenders and a tilt-cab for ease of servicing. (Doug Grieve Collection)

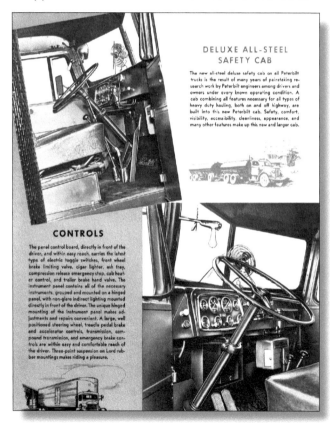

The Peterbilt COE 281 and conventional 351 models featured spacious, wide cabs and a two-piece curved windscreen for improved visibility. Production ceased in 1959. (Doug Grieve Collection)

With the arrival of the 350 conventional in 1952, series production had begun. In 1954, the model 351 was added to the line-up, and continually evolved in subsequent forms until 1976.

By the mid-fifties, the flat front 281 and 351 COE designs were offered, as well as larger models, such as the 451 COE.

Despite initial success in the fifties, a market downturn resulted in reduced sales, and Peterbilt was purchased by the Pacific Car and Foundry in 1958. In 1959, Peterbilt introduced its new 282 and 352 COE designs that proved very popular and remained in production until 1980.

The standard engine in the Peterbilt 351 conventional was the NHC-250 Cummins diesel.
(Doug Grieve Collection)

In 1959, Peterbilt introduced its new 282 and 352 COE designs, replacing earlier model 281 and 351 trucks. The 352 came in four different cab lengths, ranging from 54in to 86in, and featured dual headlamps.
(Doug Grieve Collection)

REO

REO was first established as a car company in 1904 by Ransom E Olds after he departed Oldsmobile, which he had founded back in 1897. He was not allowed to use the Oldsmobile name on this new automobile – although he tried – so he used his initials, calling the new firm the REO Motor Car Company. In 1910, the REO Motor Car Company of Lancing, Michigan introduced its first truck under the name of its subsidiary the REO Motor Truck Company. Records indicate REO had built a truck version as early as 1908 known as the model H, but the first full year of REO truck production by the subsidiary was 1911.

In 1915 REO introduced its famous Speed Wagon. The REO Speed Wagon would go on to become a legend in the truck world in North America with its continuous introduction of industry innovations, such as the fitting of pneumatic tyres, shaft-drive, electric start and electric lights, as well as being recognised for its overall robust design.

In 1949, REO restyled its longstanding truck line that first appeared a decade before. Known as the E series, the range included five 17,000 to 22,000lb GVW trucks and 22,500 38,000lb tractors. Promoted as being designed for both comfort and hauling heavier loads, the range of eleven models included five tandem units and a choice of seven different engines. In 1951, it was renamed the F series. Also new was REO's 6-cylinder, 160hp Gold Comet engine. In the 1950s, Gold Comet sixes and eights were considered some of the best powerplants in the industry. These engines would ultimately be offered in White trucks, as well. (Doug Grieve Collection)

Reo Gold Comet Truck

Compared with 5 competitive trucks, a REO Truck with Gold Comet Power hauls up to 1455 lbs. more payload per trip—earns up to $2160 more each year.

Don't wait! Let us show you the facts. Phone a REO representative NOW! Let him prove how you can earn more and save more with REO.

REO MOTORS, INC.

LANSING 20, MICHIGAN

Printed in U.S.A.—Form No. 109

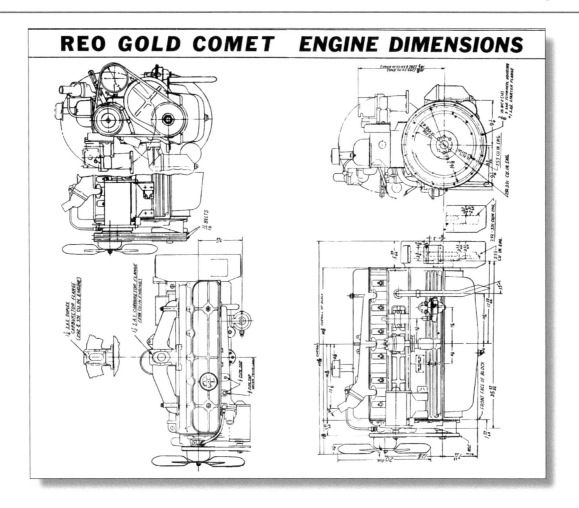

In 1953 the standard engine offered in an REO was the Gold Comet 6-cylinder. REO also offered liquid petroleum propane gas (LPG) engines in 1953 and '54, and a V8 engine in its heavy-duty trucks. By 1955, REO was offering a 100,000 mile warranty on its new 6-cylinder Gold Comet gas and LPG engines, and on its Gold Comet 195 or 220hp V8. Finally, in 1956 REO offered its first diesel engine: a Cummins turbo.
(Doug Grieve Collection)

The Speed Wagon chassis could have any number of different bodies fitted, from ambulance to hearse to school bus, as well as the various truck designs.

As the REO Lancing plant expanded, so did the company's truck line. Fifty per cent of truck production in the US in the early 1920s can be accredited to the Speed Wagon.

When the Depression hit, sales nosedived throughout the industry, and REO was no exception. Sales plummeted by 38.9 per cent by the end of 1930 compared to the previous year. REO lost money every year from 1930 to 1940, except for 1933.

By 1958 White had bought REO, and was offering the D-600 and D-700 series in six models. This is a photograph of a surviving REO A632. (Andrew Mort)

REO avoided bankruptcy thanks to a government loan, and had just began building its new line of trucks after sitting idle for 16 months when Pearl Harbour was attacked.

During the war REO built 29,000 military vehicles, yet following the war, strikes and a shortage of materials and parts hampered recovery. Still, REO carried on and introduced more new Gold Comet engine-powered models.

With the start of the Korean conflict in 1951, REO began supplying the US Army with the 2½-ton, 6x6 'Eager Beaver' or M-34 truck. Praised by both the military and the industry, orders for these trucks soon became essential in REO's survival. Yet at the

New in 1955 was the REO Super-V63 COE. Due to its compact design it could haul a 35ft trailer and still remain within the 45ft limit. A new, conventional cab B and BL series appeared in 1957, offered with a choice of nine different Cummins diesel engines ranging in power from 175hp to 335hp. (Doug Grieve Collection)

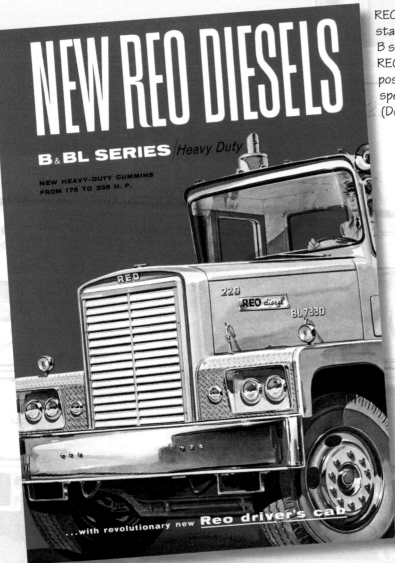

REO was the first truck manufacturer to offer standard dual headlamps; standard on the 1957 B series, with single lamps an option. In 1957, REO stated, "... over 8000 combinations are possible in custom engineering a model to your specific operating requirements." (Doug Grieve Collection)

same time, both Studebaker and GMC were building the M-34. As truck builder REO was now the tenth largest, up from eleven in 1952, but production had slipped another 2000 units to just 15,561 by 1953.

Despite more military contracts in the early fifties and attempts to diversify, REO was purchased in 1954 by Bohn Aluminum and Brass Corporation. Despite being promised a secure and long future, the Corporation sold REO in 1957 to the White Motor Company.

White established its new holding as the REO Division. White had already bought Autocar in 1953 and signed an agreement with Freightliner. (This agreement would end in 1977 and Freightliner once again became fully independent.)

In 1958 REO announced a Cseries line, but that same year White went on to buy Diamond T. Production of these trucks was moved to Lancing, Michigan, where both REO and Diamond T were built until 1966 as separate trucks. In 1967, White announced the new Diamond REO Division.

Sicard

This Canadian builder, from Ste Therese, Quebec, dates back to 1927. The company built trucks, but was a specialist in the manufacture of snow-clearing and municipal cleansing vehicles. (The company founder Arthur Sicard had invented the snowblower in 1925.) Sicard also built various series of tractor trailer units throughout its history, and despite relatively low production numbers they were a familiar sight in eastern Canada during the 1950s.

Sterling to 1953

Based on the Sternberg Motor Truck Company (1907-1915), Sterling thrived, and in 1932 purchased LaFrance-Republic Corporation, but production levels soon decreased with the continuing Depression. One of the company's projects during World War II was working with the US Army in the joint design of a heavy-duty, chain-drive, 6x6 known as the T-28.

This was followed by the T-35 and eventually the T-46 which could haul up to 75-tons (68,025kg).

The Sterling patented wood-lined, bolted frames were eventually dropped, despite the continued production of these prewar designs.

In 1951 the firm was acquired by White, but in 1953 the nameplate was dropped in favour of Autocar.

Sicards are rare, so three restored examples all from the original Miron, Quebec fleet is an exceptional sight. These T-6400 series trucks date back to the late fifties. (Doug Grieve Collection)

Following the Sterling takeover by White, the firm's models were marketed as Sterling White trucks, but were unchanged. Production continued of the division's heavy, custom-built models. In 1952 all production was transferred to White's Cleveland facility. It should be noted that in 1933 Sterling became one of the first trucking concerns to offer an optional

Studebaker

Studebaker first built electric commercial vehicles before switching to gas in 1913, but soon abandoned the market. From 1927 new buses and 1- to 3-ton (907-2722kg) trucks were gradually introduced and evolved. During the war Studebaker built 6x4 and 6x6 Hercules-powered 2½-ton military trucks.

The prewar M-types continued in production for 1946 and were joined by the Studebaker 102hp, L-head, 6-cylinder, gas-powered 2R line in 1949. A total of 67,000 Studebaker trucks were delivered in the last three years of the decade.

Throughout the 1950s Studebaker continued to focus on trucks of 2-tons (1814kg) or less, but it also built larger units such as the 2R16 rated up to 3½-tons (3176kg). Only the styling was updated and a

Studebakers hauled by a Studebaker – of course! This E series, or Transtar, was powered by a Studebaker V8.
(Doug Grieve Collection)

V8 engine offered in 1953. The E series appeared in 1955, but after 1956 the larger trucks were generally known as Transtars. In contrast to the end of the previous decade, total production annually for the last three years of the 1950s was a mere 5000 to 6000 units a year, including its popular ½-ton (454kg) pickup trucks.

White

The White Sewing Machine Company would soon abandon its steam-powered vehicles after being renamed the White Company in 1906. Production of larger, heavy-duty trucks led to its first gas-powered truck in 1910. The company flourished, and by the end of the 1930s the gas-powered line-up ranged

Introduced in 1949, the White Super Power trucks proved immensely capable, and helped the firm enter the very challenging next decade in a strong sales position. This 1951 Super Power has been completely restored. (Norm Mort Collection)

The White 3000 series Super Power COE trucks featured tilt-cabs, 2-speed rear axles, and a number of optional engines, including a 6-cylinder Cummins diesel engine. (Doug Grieve Collection)

White introduced its BBC 5000 COE series in 1959. The new short cab incorporated a fibreglass body and lightweight alloys. (Doug Grieve Collection)

from 1½-tons to 16½-tons. White built many trucks and scout cars during the war, and in 1945 resumed production of updated prewar models until 1949 when the new Super Power 3000 line was introduced. White continued to grow, first taking over Sterling and Autocar, and then later in the decade REO and Diamond T. At the same time it had an affiliation with Freightliner.

In 1955 White was offering tractors capable of hauling up to nearly 6-ton (5442kg) gross weights powered by a turbocharged Cummins diesel or a 215hp White Mustang gas engine.

In 1959 the 5000 series was introduced, featuring lightweight material, standard Cummins diesels and offered with a Clark, Fuller or Spicer transmission.

Like many truck manufactures in the 1950s, White also built buses. This stylish example is a 1957 Super Power WC22PL model. Standard features included air brakes and an 8-speed Road Ranger transmission. (Andrew Mort)

American trucks at work

Ihile the 1950s saw more and more trucks built to meet the demands of the North American market, the number of trucking companies decreased as competition became fiercer. Easy access to parts and service across the continent became more and more important.

Also, the variety of tasks and payload demands on trucks continued to increase throughout the decade.

Pictured is a beautifully restored 1956 A-603 powered by a Gold Comet 6-cylinder engine hauling a 1951 Caterpillar tractor on a 1956 Fruehauf low-bed. (Andrew Mort)

This White saw regular duty supplying materials for the first Toronto, Canada subway line, which would eventually open in March 1954. (James Sercombe)

This Autocar can be seen hauling a dozer for construction work during the postwar building boom of the 1950s. (James Sercombe)

A 1953 Federal fitted with larger west coast mirrors is transporting a house to a new location due to road widening. (James Sercombe)

In 1951, the White WC2864 was brand new, and a favourite of the owner/driver Gordon Sercombe. Here, Sercombe is transporting historic street cars for use in the upcoming Santa Claus parade. (James Sercombe)

Trucks were called on to perform a multitude of tasks. Here's another Toronto Transit Commission street car haul, but this time via a 1954 International. (James Sercombe)

Hauling logs out of northern Quebec was no easy task in the 1950s. This new, mid-fifties GMC was driven out of Lennoxville by Malcolm (Mike) Hodge. Hodge was known for straight and tidy loads; essential in the slippery, icy conditions. (Mark Hodge Collection)

Pictured in the eastern townships of Quebec in the last half of the 1950s, these GMC and Dodge trucks hauled logs – and pretty much anything else in the off-season. (Mark Hodge Collection)

American trucks, American ingenuity

New ideas & specially equipped trucks

During the jet age of the 1950s literally hundreds of new ideas and designs were unveiled.

Examples of new advances included tubeless truck tyres in 1955 and the development of the air-sprung driver's seat that lessened the fatigue level, while also providing more comfort. It was originally introduced by Bostrom in the last half of the1950s.

In 1948, 1,035,174 trucks were sold in America, but only 4485 were diesel-powered. By 1950 that figure had nearly tripled, yet still represented only 1.3 per cent of total truck production. Diesel power continued to grow in popularity, but would not become the favoured method until the 1960s. 1953 International RDF310 Cummins diesel featured. (Andrew Mort)

Taking delivery of a custom-built 1953 Federal, made in Detroit and powered by a Cummins diesel. Note the dealer sold not only Federal trucks, but also others ranging from two to six tons, as well as new British Hillmans and other Rootes cars and American Hudson models. (James Sercombe)

In 1950, Freightliner built an 800 COE with sleeper, which made it the very first intercontinental COE truck with an integral sleeper. Other firsts on the Freightliner 800 included a 10-speed transmission, an adjustable Bostrom seat, the fifth wheel installed directly on the frame without mounting plates or special crossmembers, a recording tachometer, electric sanders for slick roads, and the first standard tractor to have a 19.5in main driveline – the shortest available at the time. This was particularly important as it allowed the tractor to pull a 35ft trailer through states where there was a 45ft restriction. (Courtesy Freightliner)

Despite the increase in the number of diesel engines being offered, gasoline powerplants remained the most popular choice in North America throughout the 1950s – such as this 1950, gas-powered Mack model LJ85. (Andrew Mort)

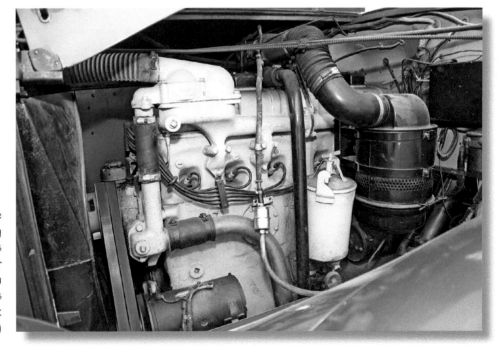

One of the many important developments in trucking in the 1950s included the introduction of the 10-speed Fuller Road Ranger gearbox with a single stick shift, and the development of a pneumatic air suspension system by Neway.

At the same time, fresh ideas such as this, introduced by smaller companies, were often greatly improved upon virtually overnight when re-invented by major competitive trucking firms.

For example, GMC's air suspension allowed for a lower floor level, and thus an additional 70ft^3 carrying capacity on a 35ft trailer.

The highly competitive truck industry was changing – and fast!

Any improvement in aerodynamics resulted in better fuel economy. The 1954 GMC 950 COE, with its high, rounded nose, proved very successful. It was this GMC model that starred in the popular television show *Cannonball*. The 1958 drama series was filmed in Canada and ran for 39 episodes. It followed the adventures of Mike Malone (Paul Birch) and Jerry Austin (William Campbell), driving their trucks across North America. (Doug Grieve Collection)

Halfway through 1953, White-Freightliner stunned the industry by introducing the first overhead sleeper cab on its dual-drive truck chassis. (Courtesy Freightliner)

REO felt it had set the 'Gold Standard of Values' in the 1950s. The company bragged of its many firsts, including the first factory engineered 6-cylinder and V8 LPG truck engines. REO was also the first to back its complete line of gas and LPG engines with a 100,000 mile warranty. (Doug Grieve Collection)

The 1953 Kenworth truck tractor CBE (cab beside engine), or Bullnose, provided excellent visibility. Some 6x4 trucks were also built. A small passenger seat was positioned directly behind the driver, and a sleeper version could also be ordered.
(Doug Grieve Collection)

The brains behind Freightliner: Ken Self (left) and Jake Jacobsen discuss cab construction. These cab panels were first hammered out by hand, but, by the end of the decade, cabs were commonly shared throughout the industry, and fibreglass was used as a lightweight alternative. (Courtesy Freightliner)

Freightliner introduced the industry's first 90-degree tilt-cab in 1958, which proved a boon in maintenance, as tasks that once took hours could be reduced to mere minutes. (Courtesy Freightliner)

By 1950 truck instrumentation had been upgraded, and continued to be improved to keep the driver better informed, as seen in this 1950 Mack LJ model 85. (Andrew Mort)

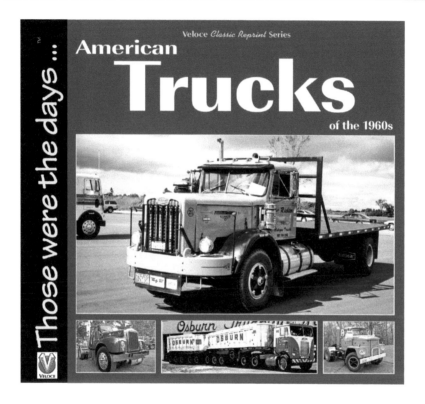

A highly visual study examines the important role of trucking in the growth of North America in the 1960s, when stiff competition led to failures and mergers.

With 120 images and evocative writing, it encapsulates the histories of the major, minor, obscure, but nonetheless historically significant truck manufacturers. Detailed captions and supportive text complement contemporary brochures, period literature, factory photos, and over fifty new, previously unpublished colour photos of restored examples to relate the importance of these historic vehicles.

ISBN: 978-1-787111-72-1

For more info on Veloce titles, visit our website at www.veloce.co.uk or www.velocebooks.com
email: info@veloce.co.uk • tel: +44 (0)1305 260068

More *Those were the days ...* titles from Veloce Publishing –

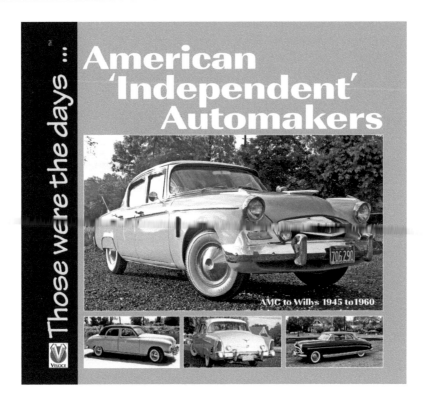

The independent automakers who had survived the depression of the 1930s had flexibility and enough capital from the war to be the first to launch all-new models for a car-starved nation. So lucrative was the American post-war car market that new automobile companies were also formed to cash in on the pent-up demand for new cars. This is their story told through text and the use of contemporary brochures, period literature, factory photos, road test info, and over 90 new, previously unpublished colour photos of restored examples to relate the importance of these historic vehicles.

ISBN: 978-1-845842-39-0

For more info on Veloce titles, visit our website at www.veloce.co.uk or www.velocebooks.com
email: info@veloce.co.uk • tel: +44 (0)1305 260068

More *Those were the days ...* titles from Veloce Publishing –

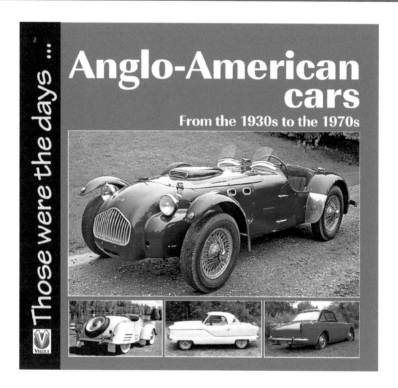

Covers British cars powered by American engines and American cars fitted with British power plants, all built from the 1930s to the 1970s. This is the first book dedicated solely to these unique hybrids bearing both American and British engineering, made for those who lust to drive something different.

Brochures, period literature, road test info of the day, factory press kits and many photos including restored examples, and detailed shots of the engines and styling that set these Anglo-American cars apart from mainstream products. Decade by decade detail allows for direct comparison.

ISBN: 978-1-845842-33-8

For more info on Veloce titles, visit our website at www.veloce.co.uk or www.velocebooks.com
email: info@veloce.co.uk • tel: +44 (0)1305 260068

More *Those were the days ...* titles from Veloce Publishing –

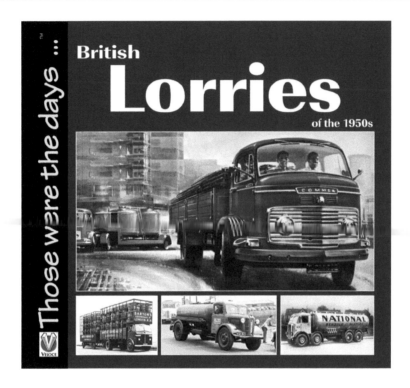

This book is a highly visual study of British lorries built during the 1950s, and contains 120 colour and black and white images, many contemporary. The photographic content extends to publicity material as well as the preservation scene depicting historic vehicles at work. All the familiar, and less familiar, names are evident, and the comprehensive text reveals much about Britain's commercial vehicle and road haulage industries, along with those marques that were household names.

ISBN: 978-1-787111-13-4

For more info on Veloce titles, visit our website at www.veloce.co.uk or www.velocebooks.com
email: info@veloce.co.uk • tel: +44 (0)1305 260068

Index

Index